STORY
BY
RICHARD C. MEYER
&
CARLOS I. SILVA

SCRIPT
BY
RICHARD C. MEYER

INTERIOR ART & BACK COVER
BY
IBAI CANALES

FRONT COVER
BY
KELSEY SHANNON

IRON SIGHTS PUBLISHED BY SPLATTO COMICS, LLC. © RICHARD C. MEYER & CARLOS I. SILVA. ALL RIGHTS RESERVED. "IRON SIGHTS," ITS LOGO, AND THE LIKENESSES OF ALL CHARACTERS HEREIN ARE TRADEMARKS OF RICHARD C. MEYER & CARLOS I. SILVA. NO PART OF THIS PUBLICATION MAY BE REPRODUCED OR TRANSMITTED, IN ANY FORM OR BY ANY MEANS (EXCEPT FOR SHORT EXCERPTS FOR JOURNALISTIC OR REVIEW PURPOSES) WITHOUT THE EXPRESS WRITTEN PERMISSION OF RICHARD C. MEYER OR CARLOS I. SILVA. ALL NAMES, CHARACTERS AND EVENTS IN THIS PUBLICATION ARE ENTIRELY FICTIONAL. ANY RESEMBLANCE TO ACTUAL PERSONS (LIVING OR DEAD), EVENTS OR PLACES, WITHOUT SATIRIC INTENT, IS COINCIDENTAL. PRINTED IN THE USA.

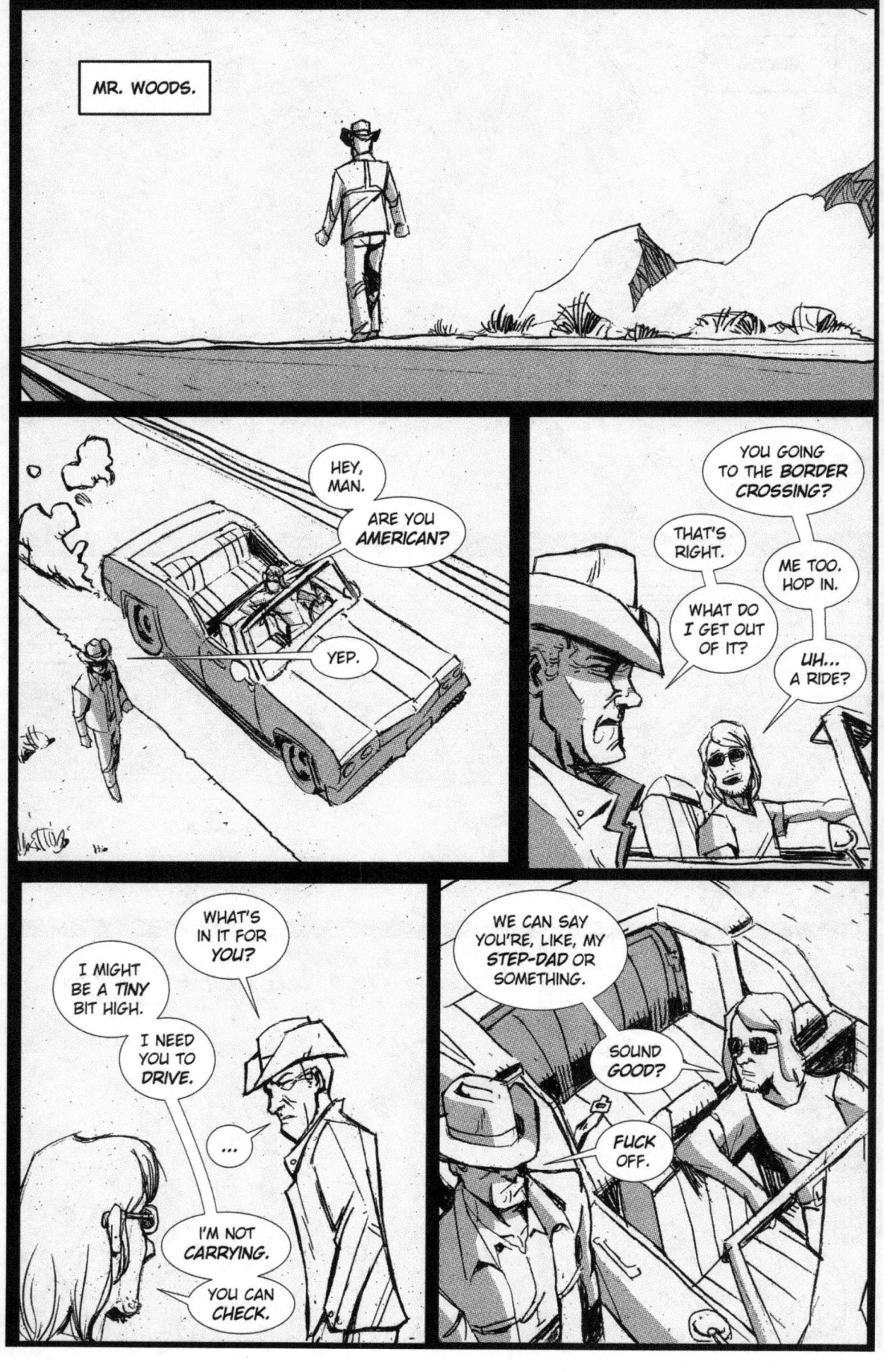

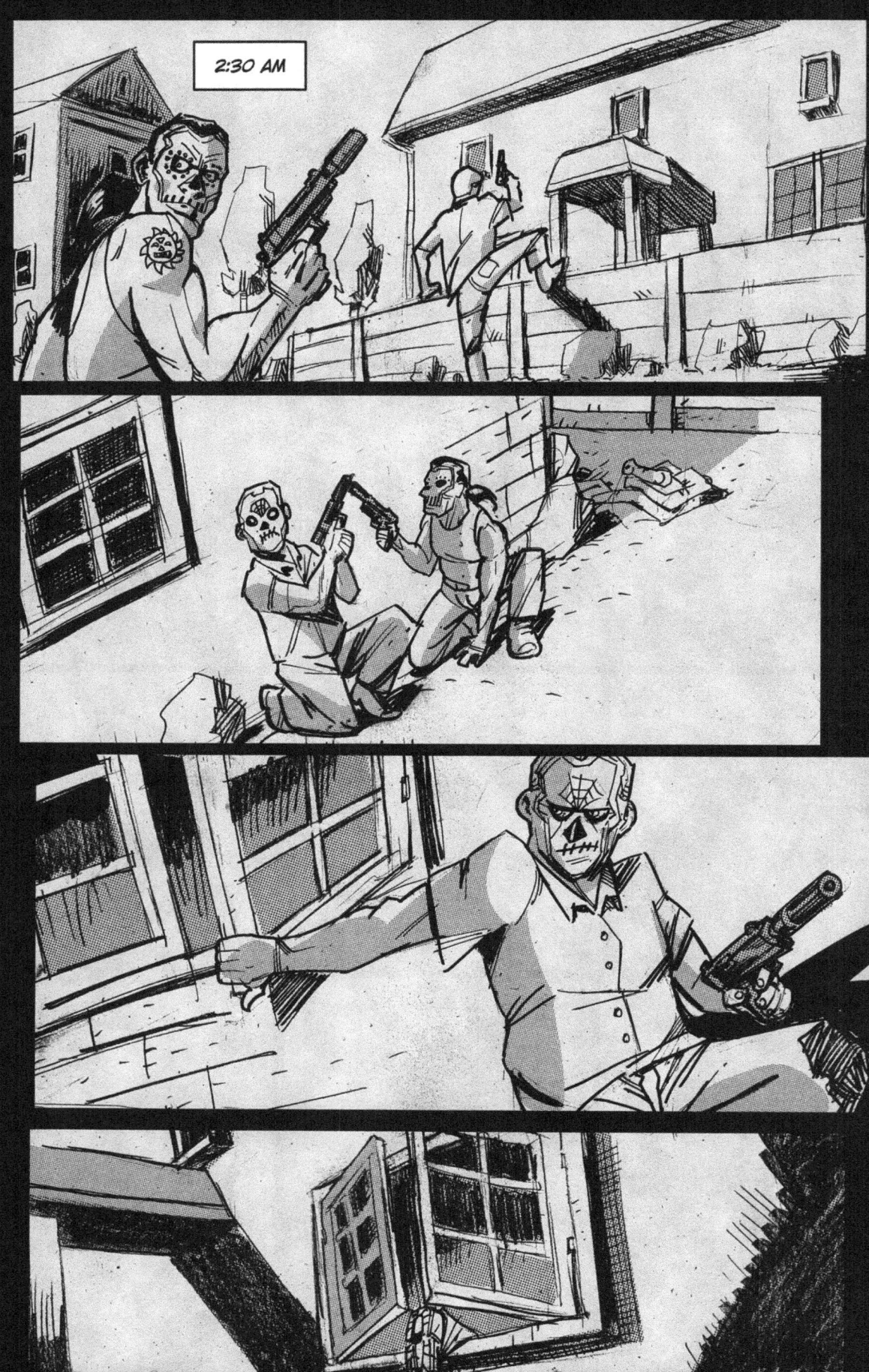

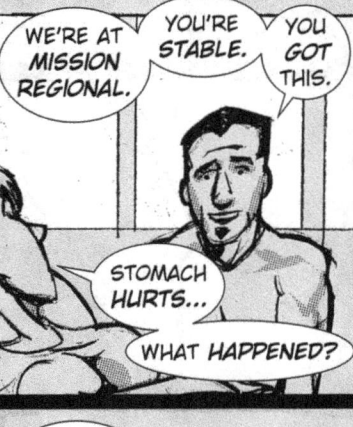

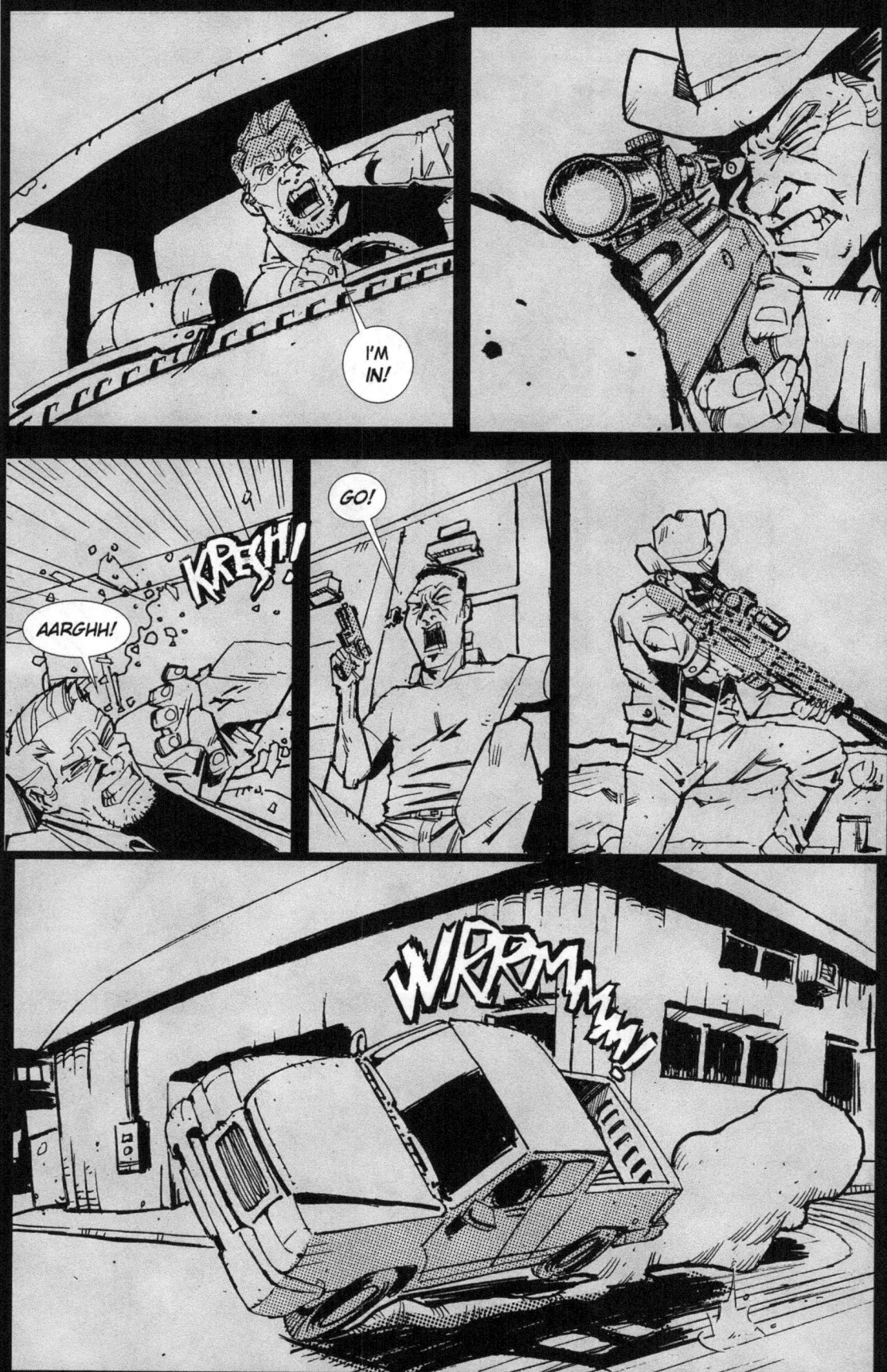

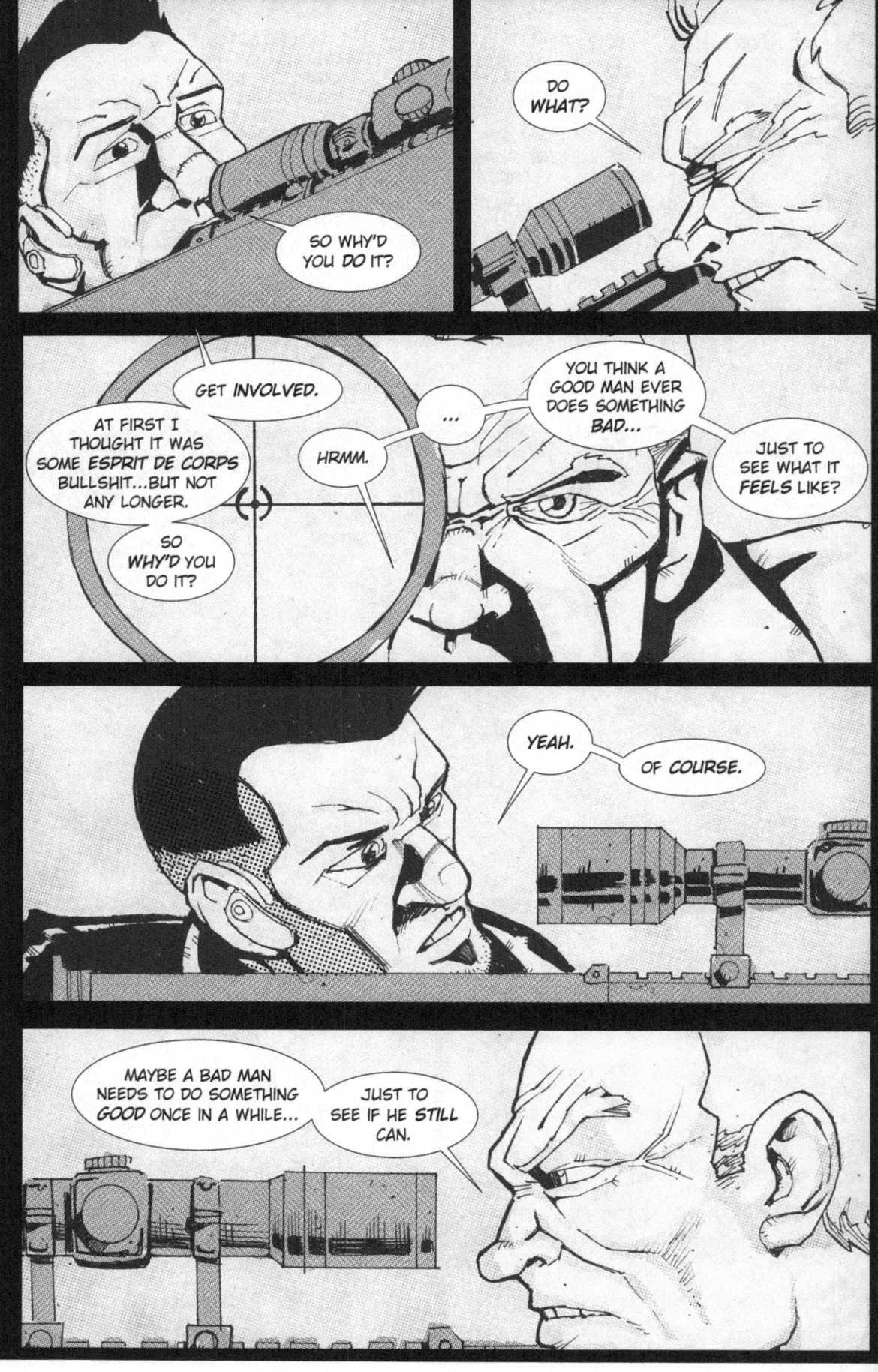

...

WOODS? WOODS!

SHIT!

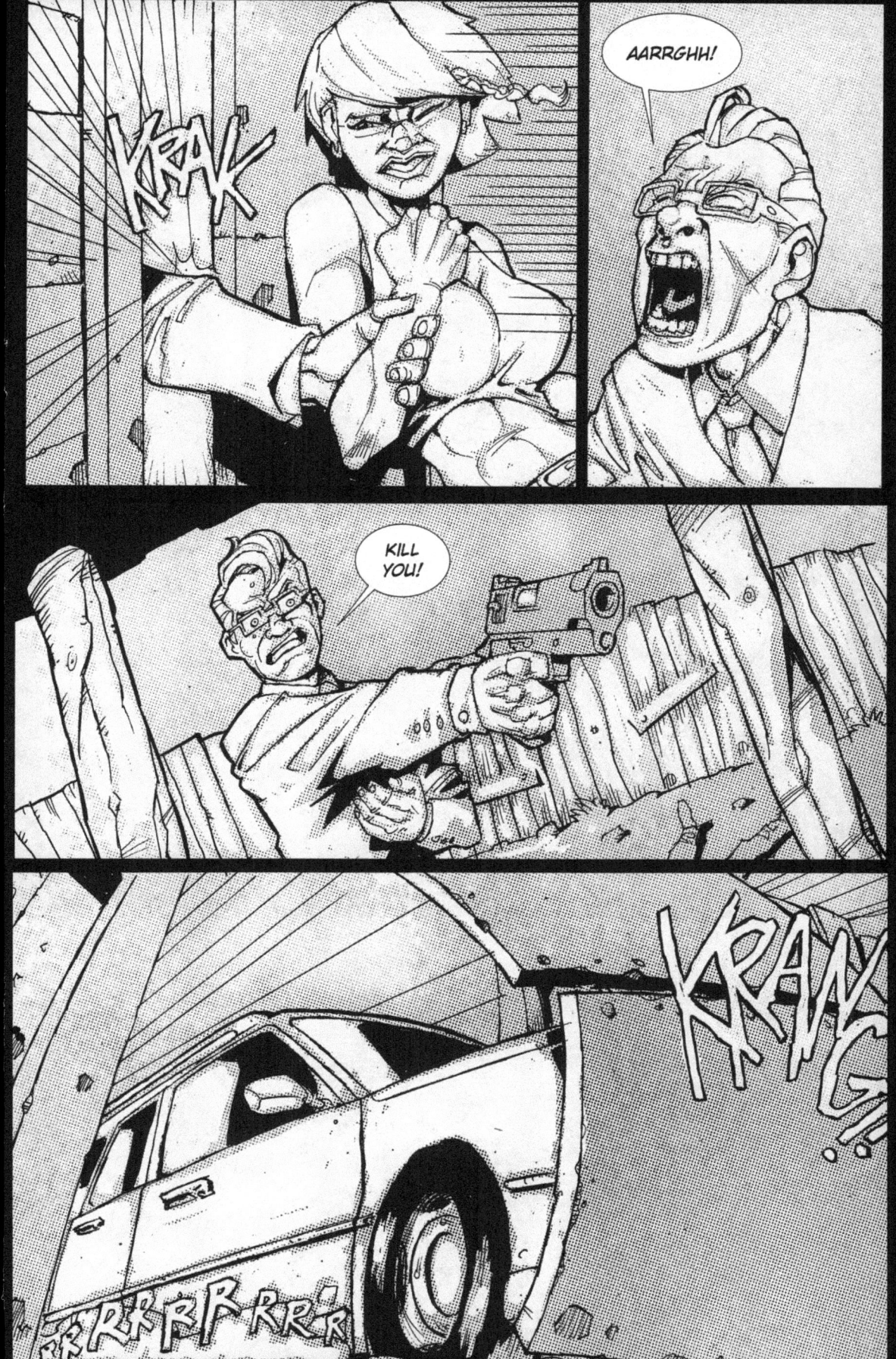

CPSIA information can be obtained
at www.ICGtesting.com
Printed in the USA
LVHW04s0016120918
589413LV00001B/1/P